SCHOOL DAZE

OVER

150

SILLY

SCHOOL

JOKES

BY

TERI JAMES-BRUMLEY

Pictures by Michael Fleishman

A TRUMPET CLUB ORIGINAL BOOK

Published by The Trumpet Club
1540 Broadway, New York, New York 10036

The trademark Dell® is registered in the U.S. Patent and Trademark Office.
ISBN: 0-440-84096-1

Printed in the United States of America
October 1989

10 9 8 7 6 5 4 3 2
OPM

CONTENTS

WARNING

READ THIS BOOK AFTER SCHOOL ONLY.
READING DURING SCHOOL HOURS MAY
BE HAZARDOUS TO YOUR HEALTH—
YOU MAY END UP LAUGHING SO HARD
THAT YOU'LL TURN RED AND BE SENT
TO THE NURSE.

CLASS PHOTOS

Arnold "The Brain" Anderson

NICKNAME: The Brain
FAVORITE CLASS: All of them
FAVORITE POSSESSIONS: His calculator and home
                    computer
FAVORITE JOKE: How many computer programmers does
                it take to screw in a light bulb?

None, that's hardware!

Jerry "The Jock" Young

NICKNAME: The Jumpin' Jock
FAVORITE CLASS: Gym
FAVORITE POSSESSIONS: His sneakers
FAVORITE JOKE: Why did the two wrestlers have to fight in the dark?

Because their match wouldn't light.

Deborah "Boy Crazy" Dalton

NICKNAME: Dating Debs

FAVORITE CLASS: History, because she heard you studied dates

FAVORITE POSSESSIONS: Bobby, Steve, Dan, Jerry, and Bruce

FAVORITE JOKE: What do you call a girl with three boyfriends named William?

A Bill collector.

Harold "Huh?" Hughes

NICKNAME: Blockhead

FAVORITE CLASS: French, because he can't understand a word the teacher says to him

FAVORITE POSSESSION: His math book, because it has more problems than he does

FAVORITE JOKE: Why is your finger in the light socket?

I'm studying current events.

Paula "Peanut Butter" Sandwich

NICKNAME: The Junk Food Junkie
FAVORITE CLASS: Lunch
FAVORITE POSSESSION: Her lunch box
FAVORITE JOKE: Why aren't elephants rich?

Because they work for peanuts.

Ben "Belushi" Berkowitz

NICKNAME: The Class Clown
FAVORITE CLASS: Geography, because he's going places
FAVORITE POSSESSION: *School Daze* by Teri James-Brumley
FAVORITE JOKE: All jokes

LOCKER LAUGHS

DATING DEBS: What are you going to be when you graduate?

JERRY THE JOCK: Very, very old.

♦

DEBS: Why does Mrs. White wear dark glasses to teach?

JERRY: Because her class is so bright.

DEBS: What does it mean if you go home and you don't have to do any chores or homework?
JERRY: It means you're in the wrong house.

◆

DEBS: When is a pink elephant most likely to enter a classroom?
JERRY: When the door's open.

◆

DEBS: When do you do your best studying?
JERRY: When my mom makes me.

◆

DEBS: I heard you're to be in my class?
JERRY: No, I'm in a class by myself.

◆

DEBS: Why is ice cream like a kid with a bad report card?
JERRY: Because they both get a lickin'.

◆

DEBS: When is a classroom door not a door?
JERRY: When it's a jar (ajar).

DEBS: Did you know that my teacher bought a dog?
JERRY: No! I thought *you* were the teacher's pet.

◆

DEBS: What are your favorite classes?
JERRY: Lunch, gym, and homeroom.

◆

DEBS: Did you study hard last night?
JERRY: Yes, during every commercial break.

◆

DEBS: What's your big sister's favorite subject?
JERRY: History! She's always making dates.

◆

DEBS: Why did Ben take his bike to school?
JERRY: Because he wanted to drive his teacher up the wall.

◆

DEBS: How is a tomato like a book?
JERRY: They're both red (read).

◆

DEBS: What did one flea say to the other flea on the way to school?
JERRY: Shall we walk or take a dog?

First Period

☆

MATH MANIA

What did one math book say to the other?

I've got problems.

◆

Why do you do your math homework with a pencil?

Because the pencil can't do it without me.

◆

How many sides does a lunchbox have?

Eight, counting the inside and the outside.

◆

How many books can you put in an empty backpack?

One. After that it's not empty.

◆

When is a table with no legs useful?

When it's a multiplication table.

What month has 27 days?

Every month.

♦

When a math teacher marries, how many husbands does she have?

Sixteen: four richer, four poorer, four better, and four worse.

♦

If I have two sandwiches and you have two apples, what do we have?

Lunch.

If you have five chocolate bars and two friends ask you for one, how many would you have left?

Five.

♦

If two's a couple and three's a crowd, what are four and five?

Nine.

♦

Why isn't your nose twelve inches long?

If it were, it would be a foot.

How much dirt is there in a hole 10 feet by 10 feet?

None (there's no dirt in a hole).

◆

When do elephants have eight feet?

When there are two of them.

◆

My math teacher flunked me again.

That figures.

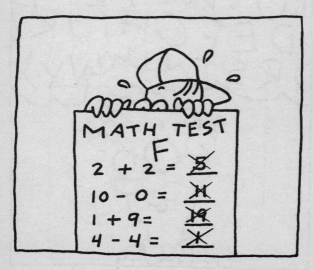

Second Period

☆

SILLY SPELLING

What did the window say when the rock went through it?

I feel fine. The pane (pain) is gone.

♦

What did the ship's captain say when the sailors jumped ship?

No crews (cruise) today.

♦

How is a man on a horse like storm clouds?

They both hold reins (rains).

♦

What did the grape say when the elephant stepped on it?

Nothing, it just let out a little whine (wine).

When do a cook's hands smell like a garden?

When they're in flour (flower).

◆

What animals are the biggest gossips?

Cats, because they can't help telling tales (tails).

◆

What fruit comes in sets of two?

Pears (pairs).

◆

Why don't soldiers eat popcorn?

Because they might eat a kernel (colonel).

◆

Why can't you whisper in school?

It's not allowed (aloud).

DELIRIOUS DEFINITIONS

What's a crowbar?

A place where crows go to drink.

♦

What do you call a cow wearing a crown?

A moo-narch.

♦

What's a small doghouse?

A pup tent.

♦

Is there such a thing as an eight-sided cat?

Sure! An octo-puss.

Why did the soldier salute the dishwasher?

It was General Electric.

♦

What monkey eats potato chips?

A chip-munk.

ALPHABET ANTICS

A

Why should the letter A be avoided?

Because it makes men mean.

B

Why is the letter B like a hot stove?

Because it makes oil boil.

C

What letter is all wet?

C (sea).

D

Why should children watch out for the letter D?

Because it makes ma mad.

E

How can the letter E keep you from getting sick?

It changes the flu to a flue.

F

When can using the letter F correctly be scary?

When it turns right into fright.

G

Why is the letter G known as the pushiest letter in the alphabet?

Because it makes O go.

H

When H meets up with this number, they become very tall.

Eight—it becomes height.

I

What two letters grow on a vine?

I & V (ivy).

J

What letter sings like a bird?

J (jay).

K

Watch out! When you add K to this word you may wind up with another cousin!

In—it becomes kin.

L

When does the letter L make a loud noise smell sweet?

When boom becomes bloom.

M & N

What letter makes N and M dangerous?

E (N-M-E—enemy).

O

The letter O and this letter feel fine together.

K (O-K—okay).

P

What two letters do the Indians use every day?

T & P (teepee).

Q

What letter is good at pool?

Q (cue).

R

Why do your friends carry the letter R around with them?

Because without it, your friends would become fiends.

S

How can the letter S make money smell like roses?

It gives a cent . . . a scent.

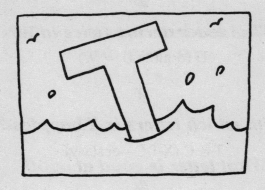

𝒯

Why is the letter T like an island?

Because it's in the middle of water.

𝒰

What is the only letter you see when looking in the mirror?

U (you).

𝒱

When coupled with this letter, V becomes jealous.

N (N-V—envy).

W

What letter occurs twice in W?

U (double U = W)

X

With which letters is X happiest?

T & C (X-T-C—ecstasy).

Y

What letter always ends a party?

The letter Y.

3

What is the simplest combination of letters?

E-Z (easy).

Third Period

☆

MUSICAL MADNESS

Bored

(To the tune of "Bad" by Michael Jackson)

As I head out the door to school,
Let me tell you true that I'm no fool.
When I get there, you know I'll find
Some teacher who will blow my mind.

It seems the same to me each day,
I wish they'd let me graduate.
It doesn't matter what the class,
You got to learn so you can pass.

Well, I know I need to learn it so I can get a job . . .
But they really make you earn it!

REFRAIN:

That's why I'm bored, I'm bored.
Come on,
You know I'm bored, I'm bored.
You know it!
Come on, I'm bored, I'm bored. You know it.
Let the whole class get to know it right now.
Let me tell you once again . . .
I'M BORED!

I watch the clock up on the wall.
The hands don't seem to move at all.
The teacher's mouth just seems to flap.
All I want to do is take a nap.

This stuff's a snooze, is my belief.
The school bell sound will spell relief.

But she keeps droning on now.
I think this class will never end.
I want to be out in the hall now
Where I can party with my friends.

REFRAIN:

That's why I'm bored, I'm bored.
Come on,
You know I'm bored, I'm bored.
You know it!
Come on, I'm bored, I'm bored. You know it.
Let the whole class get to know it right now.
Let me tell you once again . . .
I'M BORED!

Like Madonna
(the Wannabe Song)
(To the tune of "Like a Virgin" by Madonna)

On my way, off to school
I am dressed much too totally cool,
'Cuz I'm dressed just like . . .
Whoa, I'm dressed just like
My favorite star!

REFRAIN:

Like Ma-don-na!
I'm dressed in the funkiest clothes!
Like Ma-do-o-o-on-na!
There's a seam up
The back of my hose, ooh whoa ooh whoa!

Well I'm chic, it's the rule,
And the boy's think I'm nobody's fool.
And it makes me feel . . .
Whoa, it ma-a-a-a-akes me feel
Too totally cool!

REFRAIN:

Like Ma-don-na!
I'm dressed in the funkiest clothes!
Like Ma-do-o-o-on-na!
There's a seam up
The back of my hose, ooh whoa, ooh whoa!

Walk down the hall, it's a ball
'Cuz the kids they're lining the wall
Just to take a look . . .
Just to ta-aa-ake a look
At what I've got on!

REFRAIN:

Like Ma-don-na!
I'm dressed in the funkiest clothes!
Like Ma-do-o-o-on-na!
There's a seam up
The back of my hose, ooh whoa ooh whoa!

Frankie's Poodle Mandy
(To the tune of "Yankee Doodle Dandy")

Frankie's poodle went to class,
A-riding on a skateboard.
The teacher thought this really crass,
And wrote this on the blackboard:

Frankie's poodle, quite the pup!
Frankie's poodle Mandy.
Now Frankie can stay after school,
And with his pen be handy!

Pee Bee Jay

(To the tune of "Yesterday" by the Beatles)

Pee Bee Jay, that is what I had for lunch today.
And it's what she gave me yesterday.
Oh, I am sick of Pee Bee Jay.

Suddenly, lunchtime doesn't seem so good to me.
It seems I eat this stuff just endlessly.
Oh, I am sick of Pee Bee Jay.

Why it's not roast beef,
I don't know, she wouldn't say.
I said, "Something's wrong
when you dine on Pee Bee Jay."

Pee Bee Jay! Now my locker smells of Pee Bee Jay!
I'd rather smell my gym clothes any day.
Oh, I am sick of Pee Bee Jay.

Fourth Period

CAFETERIA COMEDY

PAULA: There are times when I have absolutely no appetite for food.
DATING DEBS: When do you notice this?
PAULA: Whenever I eat in the cafeteria.

◆

PAULA: What happened to the kid who ate three dozen hot dogs?
DATING DEBS: He was sick with puppy love.

◆

PAULA: I'd like my hamburger well done, please.
DATING DEBS: Our hamburgers are always done well.

◆

PAULA: When is a banana attractive?
DATING DEBS: When it's a-peeling (appealing).

◆

PAULA: What nut has no shell?
DATING DEBS: A donut.

◆

PAULA: What wobbles when it flies?
DATING DEBS: A jelly-copter.

PAULA: What makes the best slippers in the world?
DATING DEBS: Banana peels.

◆

PAULA: What did one pistachio say to the other pistachio?
DATING DEBS: I'm nuts about you.

◆

PAULA: What kind of ice did the Romans play hockey on?
DATING DEBS: Italian ice.

◆

PAULA: What did the candy bar say to the chocolate chip cookie?
DATING DEBS: You're a chip off the old block.

Fifth Period

☆

HYSTERICAL HISTORY AND GEOGRAPHY GIGGLES

Why were the Indians here before the white men?

Because they had reservations.

♦

What did George Washington's father do when George cut down the cherry tree?

Flipped his wig.

♦

Who invented the first airplane that flew backwards?

The Wrong Brothers.

♦

Where was the Declaration of Independence signed?

At the bottom.

What happened when everyone laughed at Robert Fulton's invention?

He got all steamed up.

♦

What did Cleopatra call her mother?

Mummy.

♦

What was Noah's profession?

He was an Ark-itect.

♦

What did people say when Edison invented the light bulb?

Gee, he's a bright guy.

♦

What is the difference between the North and South poles?

All the difference in the world.

What country do fish come from?

Fin-land.

♦

What country is never full?

Hungary.

♦

What would make Hungary full?

A slice of Turkey.

♦

Where can you find the Red Sea?

On Frank's report card.

Sixth Period

☆

GYM JOKES

Why is a game of baseball like a cake?

Because they both need batters.

◆

Why do professionals play baseball at night?

Because bats like to sleep during the day.

◆

Why were the gym shoes sad?

Because their father was a loafer.

◆

Why was Cinderella thrown off the baseball team?

Because she kept running away from the ball.

◆

What do you call the person who cuts the grass on a baseball field?

A diamond cutter.

Which animal hits hardest?

A bat.

♦

Did you hear a new pitcher is coming into the game?

That's a relief.

♦

I wonder why I can't learn to roller skate?

Maybe you can't get your bearings.

♦

What do a lion and a basketball have in common?

They both jump through hoops.

Seventh Period

☆

WEIRD SCIENCE AND ZANY ZOOLOGY

What did the rock say to the geologist?

Don't take me for granite.

◆

What is the most popular type of tree?

A date tree.

◆

What is the saddest type of tree?

A weeping willow.

◆

If you threw an igneous rock into the ocean, what would it become?

Wet.

◆

What is the strongest shellfish?

A mussel.

When does a bear act like your wife?

When you call her honey.

◆

What animal carries his luggage with him?

An elephant.

◆

What animals worry about their weight?

Fish—they carry their scales around with them.

What's grey, has four legs and a trunk?

Fooled you . . . a mouse going on vacation.

◆

What has four wheels and eats bananas?

A chimpanzee on a skateboard.

◆

What has four legs and flies?

A horse in the summertime.

◆

How much is a skunk worth?

One (s)cent.

◆

What two animals can open doors?

A mon-key and a don-key.

Why do birds fly south for the winter?

Because it's too far to walk.

♦

Why is it dangerous to play cards in the jungle?

Because there are too many cheetahs about.

♦

What dance do ducks prefer?

A quackstep.

♦

What do ducks like to watch on television?

Duckumentaries.

♦

How can you catch a monkey?

Hang upside down in a tree and act like a banana.

Eighth Period

☆

POP QUIZ

POP!

CLASS CLOWN IN A BOX

What never stops running all day, but goes nowhere?

A clock.

◆

What bites but never swallows?

Frost.

◆

Where does Friday come before Thursday?

In the dictionary.

◆

Why is a roomful of married couples always empty?

Because there's not a single person in it.

◆

What is full of holes but still holds water?

A sponge.

What has four eyes and runs, but cannot see?

The Mississippi River.

♦

What sees you every day, but does not know your name?

A mirror.

♦

What is the moon worth?

A dollar, because it has four quarters.

♦

What has ears but can't hear?

Corn.

♦

What has a bed, but never sleeps?

A river.

What belongs to you, but others use it more often?

Your name.

♦

What wears a coat all winter and pants in the summer?

A dog.

♦

What has many teeth but never eats?

A saw.

♦

Why is a pencil like a riddle?

It's no good without a point.

THE 10 BEST HOMEWORK EXCUSES

An alien ship visited my room last night and I gave it to them as an example of Earth intelligence.

My baby sister threw up on it.

Two gangsters in a black limousine stopped me on the way to school and said, "Your homework or your life".

A hippopotamus sat on it.

My pet boa constrictor swallowed it.

E.T. mistook it for Reese's Pieces.

I used invisible ink.

It was in the pocket of my jacket that my mom washed last night.

An elephant used it to blow his nose.

My dog ate it.

THE CLASS CLOWN

Why did Foolish Frank stand behind the donkey?

Because he thought he'd get a kick out of it.

♦

Why did Foolish Frank stand on a ladder during music class?

So he could reach the high notes.

♦

Why did Foolish Frank put ice cubes in his dad's bed?

Because he wanted a cold pop.

♦

Why did Foolish Frank look for his car in the garden?

Because he heard it just came from the plant.

Why did Foolish Frank spray insect repellent on his watch?

Because it was full of ticks.

◆

How did Foolish Frank break his leg raking leaves?

He fell out of the tree.

Why did Foolish Frank drive over the potato field with a steam roller?

Because he wanted mashed potatoes.

◆

Why did Foolish Frank take bubble gum on his vacation?

Because he heard he was going on a chew-chew.

◆

Why doesn't Foolish Frank put air in his bicycle tires?

Because he can't stand the pressure.

MORE LOCKER LAUGHS

ARNOLD: So, what did you take up in school today?
BEN: Space.

◆

ARNOLD: Why don't you like your Spanish class?
BEN: Everything is foreign to me.

◆

ARNOLD: What did the mother firefly ask her son's teacher?
BEN: Is Junior bright?

◆

ARNOLD: How many teachers does it take to screw in a light bulb?
BEN: I don't know. How many?
ARNOLD: Two. One to screw in the light bulb and one to grade her effort.

◆

ARNOLD: When do leaves begin to turn?
BEN: In the Fall?
ARNOLD: No, when the teacher announces a test.

BEN: What goes ha, ha, ha, plop?
ARNOLD: Someone laughing his head off.

◆

BEN: Knock, knock.
ARNOLD: Who's there?
BEN: Howard.
ARNOLD: Howard who?
BEN: I'm fine, howard you?

◆

ARNOLD: What did Jerry say when his father told him to stop asking for dimes?
BEN: Give me a dollar then.

ARNOLD: What does your mom do for a headache?
BEN: Sends me to the store.

◆

BEN: I gave my teacher something she'll never forget today.
ARNOLD: What, an apple?
BEN: No, a correct answer.

◆

ARNOLD: Did you have any luck in school today?
BEN: Yeah, the teacher didn't call on me.

◆

BEN: There are 15 reasons why I'm not at the top of my class.
ARNOLD: What are they?
BEN: The other kids in my class.

◆

BEN: What did the school nurse say when I told her my funny bone hurt?
ARNOLD: What?
BEN: STOP READING THIS BOOK!